Wenas in My Sketchbook

By Carleen Ormbrek Zimmerman

A selection from *The World Is a Handkerchief: Thirty Short Stories by People Like You!*

Edited by Anthony W. Parr

Ginkgo
Leaf
Publishing

Dedication

To all the authors who shared their eclectic stories,

This is for you.

To all the readers with great expectations,

This is for you.

Enjoy.

Art
"Art washes away from the soul
the dust of everyday life."
Pablo Picasso

Travel
"Like all great travelers, I have seen more than I
remember, and remember more than I have seen."
Benjamin Disraeli

Nature
"I like this place and could willingly waste my time in it."
William Shakespeare

And...life!
"You only live once, but if you do it right, once is
enough."
Mae West

Wenas in My Sketchbook

By Carleen Ormbrek Zimmerman

MY STORIES ABOUT these sketches involve my inspiration while enjoying this habitat. My excuse for sketching has always been because I am "drawn to birds." But I teach others that field sketching is not drawing. It is about using art and language to record observations. It has become my way of creating personal visual diaries of the unique habitats and experiences of our travels.

I HAVE BEEN ATTENDING the annual Wenas Audubon Campout in the Wenas Valley in eastern Washington for about 13 years. The campout was started by environmentalist Hazel Wolf, Ruth Anderson and Bea Buzzetti in 1963. It has been held every year since, except in 2020 due to the COVID-19 pandemic and in 1980 due to the eruption of Mount St. Helens.

The Wenas Valley is on the east side of the Cascade Mountains, southwest of Ellensburg and northwest of Naches. The campground lies at about two thousand feet in elevation and is surrounded by Ponderosa pine trees and wildflowers such as lupine and balsamroot. I have always been inspired by the variety of birds in the spring. I love to hear the wind whipping through the tops of the surrounding pines. It is like standing at the bottom of a river of wind. Since I live on the wet, west side of the Cascades, surrounded by Douglas firs, western red cedars and sword ferns, I love the open, dry habitats of the eastern part of Washington state.

THE FIRST SKETCH was done in 2013 on the property owned by Carolyn Comeau and Jim Leier. Carolyn inherited this historic Wenas Creek Ranch, and they have been renovating the house and property. They have offered field trips on their property every year during the annual campout. This particular field trip was for a wonderful organic breakfast that Carolyn prepared. Afterwards, we were encouraged to explore the property which is usually a wonderful place for migratory birds. I opted to sketch this beautiful old barn which used to house a stagecoach. It was a cold, cloudy, rainy day. I was thankful to be able to sketch from the covered porch. Several years later I returned to sketch the barn again on a warmer, sunny day. The constant interruptions to my field sketch that day were caused by her chickens chasing me!

THE SECOND SKETCH was done from a photo I took of my breakfast plate. Carolyn and Jim have such a unique farmhouse. I remember stained glass windows, an old Singer treadle sewing machine like my mom had in the 1950s, and an upstairs bedroom that

opened out to a deck where Carolyn would often sleep on a mattress.

The breakfast dishes were a lovely pattern of cobalt blue with a red, green, and yellow floral design reminding me of Norwegian rose painting. She made us organic scrambled eggs, sausage, roasted potatoes, and offered coffee and organic orange mango juice. Our place settings were decorated with cloth napkins and Easter Peeps. It was so delightful.

THE THIRD SKETCH, done in July 2020 during the COVID-19 pandemic, was from the area we usually camp. The campout had been cancelled.

We decided to camp there much later in the summer than we usually do. The new vault toilets put in by Department of Natural Resources remained closed due to the pandemic. We were the only campers, which was a poignant reminder of other years where we were surrounded by 100-200 other Audubon campers. We did not even hear the roar of ATVs like in years past.

The wind blew through the treetops, but at night it was so still that we could hear Common Nighthawks buzzing overhead and the faint call of Common Poorwills along the road. I wanted to illustrate how perspective gridlines could depict the campground and the placement of trees nearby and in the distance.

THE FOURTH SKETCH, of Pygmy Nuthatches nesting in the stump, was done onsite in 2009. I was sitting on a folding stool observing the pair of nesting birds. I had seen the female that morning bringing in nesting material. Later, I saw the male bringing food to her, assuming she was incubating. He fluttered his wings, and I could hear some vocalization by him. She stuck her head out and took the food. He then left and returned with more food.

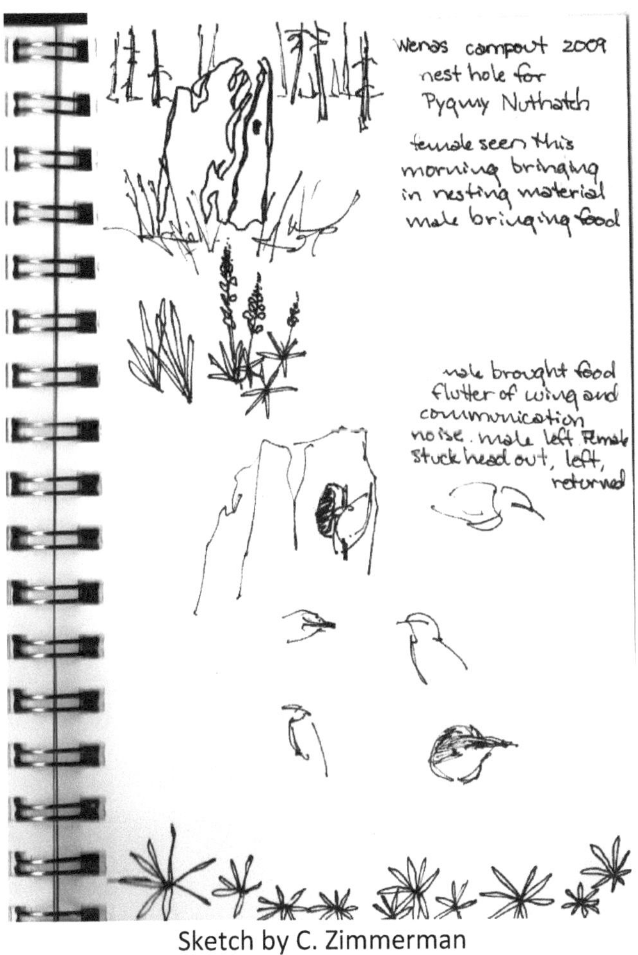

Sketch by C. Zimmerman

This stump was used for years, but I do not think there is much of it left anymore. I love doing these quick movement sketches. They capture the general impression of shape and size ("GISS"). This technique needs to be quick and spontaneous. I always use waterproof ink, which commits me to my lines. If I used pencil, I would be listening to my inner critic and constantly erasing. That would prevent me from observing. Draw what you see. Learn to look and look to learn. It doesn't have to be perfect. I also decorated the page with lupine flowers and lupine leaves, one of the most common flora in the Wenas Campground.

THE FIFTH SKETCH is of a Calliope hummingbird which I did from a photo my husband took. This bird is known to hang out along the Audubon Road as you turn right and head north from Wenas-Ellensburg Road. It is a species seen on the east side of the Cascade Mountains. Calliope hummingbirds, along with Rufous and Black-chinned hummingbirds, are common yet delightful at our hummingbird feeders we hang at our Wenas campsite. On the west side of the mountains, we only get Anna's and Rufous hummingbirds.

THE SIXTH SKETCH was done in 2015. I love to divide the page into thumbnails and depict a collage of flora and fauna, including the bird species seen and heard. In fact, over the years I have recorded so many multisensory experiences in my field sketches that they have become personal visual diaries.

These thumbnails include the intriguing pattern of the rough Ponderosa pine tree bark with the brilliant lime green lichen that covers it. The lupine blooms are a fascinating experience in watercolor mixing, requiring ultramarine blue, alizarin crimson hue, phthalo green with a touch of quinacridone burnt sienna as a complementary color to tone it down.

Lastly, Ponderosa pinecones are a constant challenge to sketch. Size and shape of petals decrease at the tip. Petal lines are slightly curved to depict the three-dimensional image of the circular cone. And the contrast of using negative space to depict the positive shapes of the petals can be overwhelming. It is always better to "undersketch," meaning sketch enough to give the impression of the cone without getting trapped in the meticulous detail. It does not have to be a scientific illustration.

THE SEVENTH SKETCH is from 2014 and is another group of thumbnails. I chose to include the nest box on a Ponderosa pine tree near us in the campground that was being used by a pair of Mountain Bluebirds. Another thumbnail was of the Ponderosa pine branch where we hung our hummingbird nectar feeder, which immediately attracted Rufous, Calliope and Black-chinned hummingbirds. The third thumbnail was off the much-appreciated porta-potties which the Wenas Audubon committee rents for the campout.

The campout is on Department of Natural Resources land which allows dispersed camping. There are no facilities or water provided. Campfires are not permitted, but law enforcement rarely appears on site during the Memorial Day weekend. If they do, they seem to issue more tickets to ATV drivers riding without helmets or driving too fast. The porta-potty sketch, by the way, became a useful reference for me when I later became co-treasurer and responsible for reserving the porta-potties. I could not remember the name of the company. Suddenly, I remembered my sketch and was glad I had included the company name, Valley Septic. I googled them, called them up to make the reservation, and thanked them by sending my sketch of their porta-potties at the campout. They thought that was hilarious!

THE EIGHTH SKETCH was done in 2013 and is a typical view of a Wenas campsite. It includes someone's tent, someone else's trailer, porta-potties, a hummingbird feeder on a Ponderosa pine, and lupine. That is the campout habitat in a nutshell.

THE FIRST YEAR WE ATTENDED the Wenas Campout was in 2006. We volunteered on the spot to lead activities. While my husband led the owl prowl and other birding trips along Wenas Creek, I offered to hold field sketching. I had one person on Saturday afternoon who wanted to learn about sketching equipment in the field. And I had one person on Sunday afternoon who was a native plant naturalist who was interested in drawing flora. Since 2006, I have offered field sketching two times every year at each campout. I have had 20-30 people in a session. Many people have returned to sketch with me every year. Some children have enjoyed sketching with me and come to expect the activity, hanging out until I begin the session. It has been a joy to inspire others and share how I appreciate the natural environment.

Afterword *by Anthony W. Parr*

When I attended my first Wenas gathering it was a privilege to join nature's sister, Hazel Wolf, on a wildflower hunt.

I also was with Carleen at the Creek Ranch, a wonderful home with generous hosts. I ate the same breakfast that Carleen sketched. It tasted as good on the lovely plates as Carleen's sketch depicts.

I just was looking through a lovely book by Constance Sidles, Fill of Joy, *and there was a sketch by Carleen. And one by me, that Constance had added to her tale of birds and people at the Montlake Fill in Seattle, Washington.*

Praise for

The World Is a Handkerchief

Of the 30 stories, I am especially enchanted by two about being a gardener. Growing up in Michigan, Colleen M. Donahue was surrounded by plants and gardens as a child. As an adult, managing the Master Gardeners' display and teaching garden in Bellevue, she has learned there is so much more to being a gardener. "Growing A Gardener" shares not only techniques, but also the many ways cultivating plants enriches the lives of all beings, especially humans. Maybin tells a similar story, but from a very different cultural starting point in Zambia. "Maybin's Garden" uses a conversational presentation style and includes vibrant drawings of the garden space. I found that both writers captured the essence and spirit of gardening in ways that were very relatable and inspiring.

--Brian Thompson, Manager of the Elisabeth C. Miller Horticultural Library, University of Washington Botanic Gardens

***

I am grateful for your wonderful book - just reading about the woodcutter from Lake Wilderness.

Emerson once wrote: "Live in the Sunshine, Swim in the Sea, Drink the wild Air."

When you share stories with us, I feel as though we all get to partake in Emerson's world!

--Lori Carmody

***

I loved reading about "the world is a handkerchief" explanation! I like this idea of threads interlining just as our lives do with other people.

I also loved reading about the flower displays! Maybe it'll inspire me to start my own flower garden! It was very nice reading how passionate the person telling the story was about it.

--Maria Jose Felix, Composer/Sound Designer at SkyRoseMusic

***

I really enjoyed reading Wenas in My Sketchbook. I was transported to the campground through the author's writing. The sketches accompanying the stories were also very enjoyable.

--Raghav Mehta, Bird Photographer and Audubon Trip Leader

***

What an interesting, vivid account [Three Lessons on the Path to Enlightenment] told with the ability of understanding and embracing the characters in their environments and landscape surroundings. Only an acute observer can describe the moment with clarity and wisdom.

--Elfi Rahr

***

My! Oh! My! What a gift!

I held the book close to my heart, a little emotional and then my heart got bubbly excited. Tony, your heart gift landed in two grateful hands and as expected, my heart smiled heartily. The journeys, the details, the experiences around the world are all blending together in my heart.

Why aren't they more human beings like Tony, I asked myself? Then the world will be far richer and better. No sooner than I asked that question, I heard a whisper in my heart. "The stories are saying look closely, there are many Tony's dressed in different garments. The book, the stories, are seeds Tony gathered along the way and freely shared to give evidence of deep, deep hope. One man's journey becomes the tillage of the heart from which all arts follow. It's like many incredible movies weaved together to make a masterpiece. Thank you, Tony, for gathering us together to shine a spotlight on the essence of humanity. You've handed a torch light to me, to go further in my life work of tending the garden. I shall hold soil and seed tightly close to my heart.

You've also given me new members of the family by weaving all these stories together. This summer I'll sit in the garden and read these stories to children and their parents. The thirty stories will then become many stories.

--Maybin Chisebuka, The Amazing Gardener

***

Tony, reading your Elvis story sparked my own fond memories of my mother and her love for Elvis, and my own love for her and his music. Through the years my flavor of rock and roll strayed a long way from what my mother would accept as music but we always could agree on Elvis. I got my guitar when I was nine and the first thing I did was run around the house imitating the king. My mom passed away of cancer in 2018 in what turned out to be a very sad chapter in my life. Shortly after she got sick, but had not told me yet, she sent me her original pressing of Blue Hawaii, all 14 songs. I can

see her dancing in the living room of the old house every time I play this album. It still brings tears to my eyes as I write this but I will forever be grateful to my mom and Elvis for filling my heart with the love of rock and roll.

--Don Sanders, Investor, Musician and Desert Dweller

ABOUT THE EDITOR

Anthony W. Parr is an Author, Illustrator, and Artist.

This collection, The World is a Handkerchief, is the first book he has compiled and edited.

Somewhere near Casa Grande is his first Illustrated story book, with a series to come.

Many poems, eulogies, letters, and stories have flowed from Parr's pen.

His artwork includes pen drawings of many famous

authors, in situ, at book events,

and charcoal drawings of theatrical artists and

acts in action.

Wide-ranging plein air drawings in the desert,

at the seaside,

and in the countrysides of England, Germany, France,

Italy, Australia, and the US.

Oil paintings and watercolors of grand visions in

Milan, Chaing Mia, and Athens.

OTHER BOOKS BY ANTHONY W. PARR

Somewhere Near Casa Grande

When a fox named Fresno encounters three border-crossing foxes from Mexico, they all wind up partying at a palm oasis—in a series of enchanting illustrations by British-born artist **Anthony W. Parr**. "A fox knows no borders, just how to have a good time in the desert," proclaims this parable, available now on Amazon in English and Spanish.

Parr's first book, *Somewhere Near Casa Grande*, shows his talent as a desert artist who has extensively hiked and painted near his part-time home in Palm Desert (he lives the rest of the year in Bellevue, Washington), as well as the backcountry near Tucson where his tale is set.

The book was inspired by his daughter **Kristina Parr** ("Why don't you write about foxes?") and is the first of several from his own Ginkgo Leaf Publishing company.

Parr tells readers of **California Desert Art** that he will send a free copy to teachers or anyone wishing to learn the fate of the furry comrades.

Email: tony@machinesandmethods.com

Review by Ann Japenga in California Desert Art Newsletter.